Time Management and Personal Development

John Adair
and Melanie Allen

HAWKSMERE

© John Adair and Melanie Allen 1999

Published by Hawksmere plc
in association with Filofax

Hawksmere plc
12-18 Grosvenor Gardens
London SW1W ODH
0207 824 8257

Designed and typeset by Paul Wallis for Hawksmere

A CIP catalogue record for this book is available from the British Library.

ISBN 1 85418 182 3

Printed in Great Britain by Ashford Colour Press.

Contents

Part 1

Time Management

Philosophy

1 Develop a personal sense of time

2 Identify long-term goals

9 Make use of committed time

10 Manage your health

Part 2

Personal development

Philosophy

5   Your personal profile

About this book

Time Management and Personal Development stands out from other books in an important way. It is a book to use for your own self-development.

This guide can be used in several ways. Here are the main possibilities to consider:

▶ **Individual study.** This book is a complete method of self-teaching

▶ **Workshops and seminars.** It can be issued to all participants well in advance of a seminar or course. More time can then be spent in the seminar exchanging users' experience and discussing practical applications. The book is also a workbook that can be given out at the beginning of a seminar, with participants completing some of the exercises and checklists as the programme unfolds

▶ **Distance or open learning.** The book can be part of an organisation's distance learning strategy, covering those who, for one reason or another, will not be able to attend seminars or workshops.

What are your objectives?

Time management and personal development is a very personal affair. We all have different needs, interests and priorities.

Give some thought to what particular **benefits** or **outcomes** you are hoping for from working through this book. What in particular are you trying to accomplish?

Please put a number beside each of the benefits and outcomes below: 1 (vital), 2 (desirable), 3 (low priority).

By completing this book I intend to:

▶ Organise my day more effectively

▶ Link up my long-term and middle-term objectives with my daily action planning

▶ Identify and control the major time-wasters in my life

▶ Improve the quality of my working time

▶ Recognise and value past and present achievements

▶ Identify transferable skills and personal competence

▶ Clarify personal and professional goals

▶ Assess strengths and weaknesses in my range of competences

▶ Collect evidence for a portfolio of achievements

▶ Form clear development objectives

▶ Set up a development action plan

▶ Collect together evidence and information for a personal profile.

one
Time management

'Nothing really belongs to us
but time, which even he has
who has nothing else.'

Baltasar Gracian

'Time wasted is
existence, used is life.'

Edward Young

Philosophy

Towards a new philosophy of management

What is your role as a manager? What do you consider to be your core responsibilities?

These are fundamental questions. The answers you give will form a substantial part of your own personal philosophy of management.

Managers at all levels are business leaders. The business (literally the area in which one is busy) is about producing quality products or services at a profit (or at least in the most cost-effective way).

At the heart of that role lie the three overlapping core responsibilities of any leader:

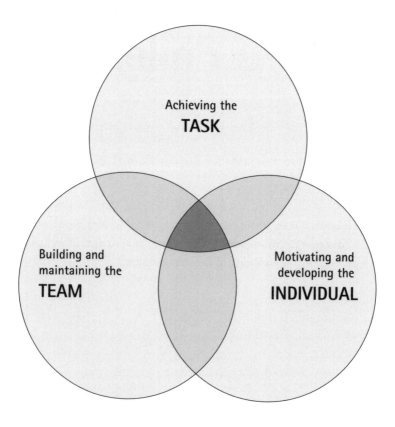

Achieving the
TASK

Building and
maintaining the
TEAM

Motivating and
developing the
INDIVIDUAL

This model implies an understanding of the environment in which one is working, as well as the need to possess or develop the necessary qualities of personality, character, and skills to provide the necessary leadership functions – defining the objective, planning, briefing, controlling, informing, supporting and reviewing.

The three circles model of leadership functions integrates together what we customarily call leadership and management. But these concepts do retain some distinctive overtones:

LEADING is about	MANAGING is about
Giving direction, especially in times of change.	Running the business in 'steady state' conditions.
Inspiring or motivating people to work willingly.	Day-to-day administration.
Building and maintaining teamwork.	Organising structures and establishing systems.
Providing an example.	Controlling, especially by financial methods.
Producing a personal output.	

Both sets of skills and abilities are essential. You have to be a manager-leader or a leader-manager depending on your specific role and/or level of responsibility in the organisation.

The leader-manager-professional concept

You may also have to combine with these core abilities a professional area of responsibility, such as working as an engineer or accountant. Thus there are often three elements in our jobs – managing, leading and professional – which vary in proportion as our career develops. The actual shape of the triangle in your role circle below, will alter as your responsibilities develop or unfold.

This particular concept or philosophy of leadership/managership places a very high premium on you being able to manage your time well. This is easier said than done. For, apart from the core responsibilities of leadership, which invariably means spending lots of time with people both in groups and as individuals, there are all the other demands of running a business or part of one. Information technology and financial management systems can help here, but are only part of the solution.

Moreover, 'outside the egg' – beyond the organisation – there are customers or suppliers to be seen, conferences to be attended, networks to link into and so on. Add to that our personal needs to spend time with families and friends, in creative and re-creative activities, and you can see why the management of time becomes such a critical factor in your life.

To value time as your most precious commodity – to be spent both carefully and generously should be an essential element in your philosophy of life.

What is time?

It may seem odd to suggest that you should have a philosophy of time, for no one has ever really defined it. As St Augustine remarked long ago, 'I know what time is until someone asks me.' Where the great minds of the world have failed we are unlikely to succeed.

But we do *know* what time is. We experience it. We measure it. As it is invisible and indefinable we use metaphors to grasp some of its aspects. Time is money – yes, it is a limited and valuable resource, but it is actually more precious and cannot be stored in the bank. Time is our lives as measured out in years, months, days, hours, minutes and seconds. What could be more important to you than using this free gift of time effectively, generously and wisely?

Can you manage time?

To manage means to control. It comes from the Latin word *Manus*: a hand. The French developed Manage for handling war horses (what we now call dressage). It was soon applied to handling other things (shops, tools, money).

In modern use *managing* implies:

Efficiency
Ensuring that things or organisations run smoothly, like high-performance machines.

Effectiveness

Being economical and prudent about the use of means (resources) to accomplish ends.

It is the second aspect of managing that concerns us most here. Obviously you cannot control time in the sense of stopping it, slowing it down or speeding it up. But you can apply it economically to the tasks you have to accomplish.

Can you lead time? Again, obviously not, for time cannot be led by the hand. But we talk about someone leading their lives. Lead comes from the old North European word for a journey, road, path or course of a ship at sea. You can navigate both your life and the work that you are doing by identifying your values, aims and objectives.

Checklist – is your philosophy clear?

All navigators need some stars to steer by. Have you successfully carried out some fundamental thinking about your own key values?

▶ Write down a brief description of your role at work as a professional/manager/leader

▶ Do you accept that if you are in a position requiring leadership, you need time to think about the task, the team and each individual?

▶ Does your philosophy of business include a clear understanding of the corporate purpose?

▶ Have you thought through the ethical implications and social responsibilities of your role as a leader-manager?

▶ Have you worked out a proper and healthy balance for yourself between your professional life and commitments on the one hand, and your personal and family life on the other?

Summary

Are you convinced that time is your most precious resource? Are you persuaded that it is possible to manage time? Have you linked these beliefs to a wider **philosophy** of work, and in particular your own role as a **leader, manager** and **professional** (not necessarily in that order)?

If your answer is **YES**, then it makes sense to develop or adopt a **framework** for effective time management:

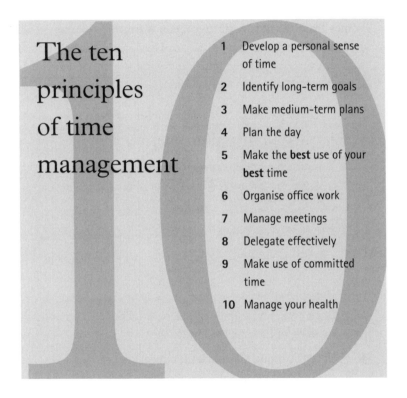

The ten principles of time management

1 Develop a personal sense of time

2 Identify long-term goals

3 Make medium-term plans

4 Plan the day

5 Make the **best** use of your **best** time

6 Organise office work

7 Manage meetings

8 Delegate effectively

9 Make use of committed time

10 Manage your health

Into this **framework** you can fit all the existing practical advice, techniques and tips on time management. You can add to them as you continue along the path of self-improvement.

Develop a personal sense of time

The best way to develop a personal sense of time is to reflect –
like Persian mystic, Ulwais the Sufi quoted below – that it is one
of your most precious resources and that it is not to be taken for
granted.

A vital difference

Ulwais the Sufi once was asked, 'What has brought grace to you'?

He replied, 'When I wake in the morning I feel like a man who is not
sure he will live till evening'.

Said the questioner, 'But doesn't everyone know this'?

Said Ulwais, 'They certainly do. But not all of them feel it'.

Everyone knows that time is limited, but few are aware of that fact.

Keeping a time log

One important way by which you can develop a personal sense
of time is to keep a time log, recording how your time is actually
spent over a period of say, a week.

The principle of a time log or audit is to divide each day for the
next week or two into fifteen minute intervals. At the end of each
hour record how the previous hour was spent.

Keeping a time log may sound to you like a tedious chore, but there
is a reason for it. There is often a gap between what we think we
are doing and what we are actually doing. Why not take an objective or experimental approach, like that of a scientist, to find out
where your time is really going? You may be in for some surprises.

Exercise

Keep a time log with you for the next week and record how each hour was spent. Be honest. If your fifteen minute coffee break turns in to thirty minutes, log it. You need to know where your time is going.

At the end of the day summarise the time spent. After keeping the logs for three or four days you may begin to notice opportunities for improvement. Could some tasks be delegated? What would happen if they were not done at all? Are you giving the really important tasks the correct priority?

Having identified how your time is truly spent you can then proceed to invest it more beneficially for the future.

How do you value other people's time?

Developing a personal sense of time includes developing a personal sense of the value of other people's time. How do you rate as a manager – or mismanager – of other people's working capital of time? To discover your attitudes to other people's time, complete the following exercise. If a statement describes your attitude or behaviour check Yes if not, check No. Tell the truth!

Attitudes and behaviours to other people's time

1. I look upon the time of those who work for me as an extension of my own, to do with as I please.

2. I frequently interrupt meetings in their offices, as I have first priority on their time.

3. I regard job descriptions – that each position in an organisation has its own proper duties, responsibilities and authority – as a bureaucratic nonsense.

4. When telephoning anyone I never check to see if my call is an unwanted interruption at that particular moment.

5. I enjoy the sound of my own voice and I know that I am rather long-winded at meetings.

6. In the last month I can think of at least one occasion when I have kept someone waiting needlessly without telling them why.

7. I am aware of the quantity of time that my people put into their work (how many hours a day), but not the quality of the time they give.

8. I have never reflected on the fact that other people's time is as precious to them – or ought to be – as my time is to me.

9. I do not show potential or actual customers that I value their time. It's their money I am after!

10. I frequently miss agreed deadlines, I say that I will do things and then don't do them, and have to be chased by others accordingly.

The following scale will help you to interpret your present level of personal awareness of other people's time based on your current attitudes and behaviours:

'No' answers

8-10 You are sensitive and thoughtful. Keep it up!

5-7 You are very good, but in some respects could be better.

2-4 Get some feedback and advice from friends and colleagues.

0-1 Beyond redemption! A radical self-review of your attitude is needed.

Summary

▶ Time – human time – is the most precious natural resource you have.

▶ Time is well-managed if:

   –   things that ought to run smoothly are doing so

   –   desired ends are being achieved by the economical use of time.

▶ Time is well-led if those ends are carefully thought through in terms of purpose, aims and objectives in a rapidly changing world.

▶ Your personal sense of time should include an awareness of the value or importance of other people's time as well as your own.

Identify long-term goals

There are basically two ways of thinking about the results or end points towards which you have chosen to direct your activity. The first ranges them from the **particular** to the **general**. The second method groups them according to **time** – from **short-term** through to **long-term**.

Example of particular to general

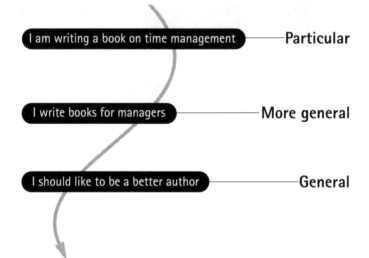

I am writing a book on time management ——— Particular

I write books for managers ——— More general

I should like to be a better author ——— General

Example of short-term to long-term

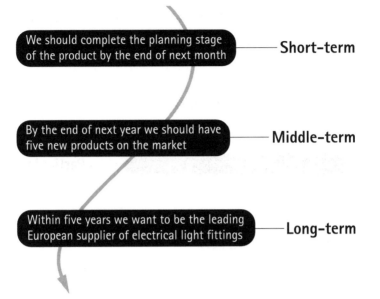

We should complete the planning stage of the product by the end of next month ——— **Short-term**

By the end of next year we should have five new products on the market ——— **Middle-term**

Within five years we want to be the leading European supplier of electrical light fittings ——**Long-term**

Obviously there is some flexibility in these time-related terms: what is long-term for some managers would be middle-term for others.

Ten key words for time planners

The English language is not a great help when it comes to thinking clearly in this area. There are a variety of over-lapping words, but they have overtones, so choose your words carefully! Here are some of the runners:

Term	Suggests
1 Purpose	Either a resolute, deliberate movement towards a result or the desired result itself. Conveys too, the idea of significance or meaning.
2 Goal	A deliberately selected result that can be won only with difficulty by dedicated and prolonged effort. In a vague sense: the general trend a person or group takes.
3 Aim	A mark or target to be aimed at, thus an object or purpose. The purposive directing of effort.
4 End	The intended effects of actions often in distinction or contrast to means.
5 Object	May equal end but often applies to a more individual determined wish and may nearly mean motive.
6 Objective	Something tangible, specific and immediately attainable, towards which effort is directed.
7 Mission	A task assigned or undertaken. The purpose for which one was sent. (Mission comes from the Latin verb 'to send'.)
8 Plan	Sets of ideas developed to accomplish a desired result. The most informal and the most general of a set of such words: blueprint, design, programme, proposal, scheme.

9 Vision	Unusual discernment or foresight/sharpness of understanding. A mental concept of a distinct or vivid kind; a highly imaginative scheme or anticipation.
10 Intention	Little more than what one has in mind to do or bring.

First define your purpose

Many organisations today have found that it makes sense to define their purpose or mission.

A proper statement of corporate purpose (as I prefer to call it) should answer the questions:

▶ Why does this particular organisation exist?

▶ To what end is all the effort and time being expended?

Wording a statement of corporate purpose that is both simple and inspiring is no easy matter. It also needs to answer the basic philosophical questions, that both takes into account and yet transcend the particular interests of the various stakeholders, and reflect the core ethical stance of the organisation. What we must be clear about however is the answer to the question.

To what end is all the effort and time being expended?

The purpose of this organisation is ....

....

The purpose of my job is...

....

Then define your strategic aims

How far you tend to look ahead in organisations depends roughly upon your position. It is the responsibility of strategic leaders to ensure that their organisations are taking a longer-term view. That involves thinking hard about these questions:

1. Where are we now?

2. What are our present strengths and weaknesses?

3. Where do we want to be in (say) five years time?

4. How are we going to get there?

5. How can we improve general capabilities?

This kind of strategic thinking (which applies to personal life as well) will tend to give you either a **direction** (or set of directions) in which you should be going, or a **goal** (or set of goals).

Example

'Our aim is to move up-market into the higher price range of package holidays'.

'Our goal is to take over ownership of The Times by the year 1999.'

As a principle, the further you look ahead the more likely you will be thinking in terms of directions or aims rather than goals or objectives. For the further away it is, the less likely you are to hit a precise target. This is equally true of course in your career and personal life. On the other hand, if you are not successful in turning your corporate (or personal) purpose into more definite directions or aims, clearly identified as being worthwhile (= worth time and effort), and then converting those into much more tangible **goals**, **targets** or **objectives** you will be nothing but a manager of good intentions.

The next section explains **how to do it.**

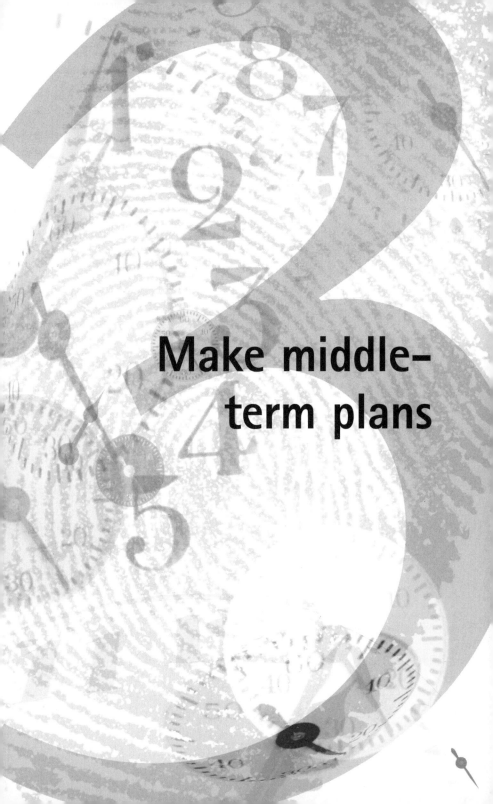

Make middle–term plans

Now you have come this far it should be fairly easy for you to identify the five or six **key areas** (as a rule of thumb – not less than three, not more than seven) of your job.

List these below:

1. ....

2. ....

3. ....

4. ....

5. ....

6. ....

7. ....

Key areas – a definition

A key area is a major sub-section of your overall job for which you are responsible. It is an area in which your performance will be directly or indirectly measured. A good indicator of your key areas will be your job description but remember apart from the obvious ones, it can also include things such as staff development.

In each of these key areas you need next to define or set **objectives**. (You may have done so already, at least partially. If so, check them). That will give you a list of objectives for the middle-term as it makes sense to define it in your job.

Check understanding

Write down one of your objectives:

....

....

....

....

....

Now turn to page 26 and check your skill in setting objectives.

It is often a good idea to make a 'time budget' for your objectives. You have only 168 hours each week. A most common mistake in time management is to underestimate the time it will take you to achieve a particular result. With practice and experience you should be able to forecast realistically and accurately how much of your time a job will take.

The progress review

At the end of the middle-term (however long that may be – three, four, six or twelve months) you should review your performance. On the time front be especially watchful for excuses, as opposed to real reasons, as to why results were not achieved.

The ability to review or evaluate your own work critically against the objectives you have set yourself is vitally important for your self-development as a leader/manager. It is not incompatible, of course, with having appraisal interviews with your boss. Indeed, research shows that the most effective appraisal interviews are those:

▶ Where prior objectives have been set and agreed.

▶ Where a measure of self-evaluation precedes the evaluation by others.

Checklist – is it a 'SMARTER' objective?

Tick box if your objective meets the criterion:

Specific	☐	Measurable	☐
Agreed	☐	Realistic	☐
Time–bound	☐	Evaluated	☐
Reviewed	☐	Strategic	☐
Meaningful	☐	Attainable	☐
Rewarding	☐	Team building	☐
Empowering	☐		

The Lord said unto Noah

The Lord said unto Noah 'Where is the Ark I commanded you to build?'. And Noah said 'Verily I have had three carpenters off sick. The gopher wood supplier hath let me down; yea even though the gopher wood hath been on order for nigh upon twelve months. The damp course specialist hath not turned up'.

And God said unto Noah 'I want the Ark finished before seven days and seven nights'. Noah said 'It will be so'.

But it was not so. The Lord said to Noah 'What seems to be the trouble this time?' Noah said 'My subcontractor hath gone bankrupt; the pitch for the outside of the Ark hath not arrived, the glazier departeth on holiday to Majorca, yea even though I offered him double time. Shem hath formed a pop group with his brothers Ham and Japeth. Lord I am undone'.

And the Lord grew angry and said 'What about the animals? Two of every sort I have ordered to come to be kept alive; where for example are the giraffes?' And Noah said 'They have been delivered to the wrong address but they should arrive by Friday.' And the Lord said to Noah 'Where are the monkeys and the elephants and the zebras?' And Noah said 'They are expected today.'

And the Lord said 'How about the unicorns.' And Noah wrung his hands and wept; 'Oh Lord, they are a discontinued line. Thou canst not get unicorns for love or money. Thou knowest how it is.' And the Lord said 'Noah my son – as a manager though art charged with achieving results. It pleaseth me not to get excuses.'

Improving time norms

Most of us know Parkinson's Law – namely that work expands to fill the time available for it. It's a good thing from time to time to look at the more routine or mundane activities involved in the smooth operation of any organisation, for example how long it is taking to invoice customers, or answer letters, or circulate information. It is all to do with **cost** and **quality** – two of your vital concerns as a manager.

While that idea is fresh in your mind, list down on the table opposite some candidates for improved efficiency.

Customers are people who come back to you for goods or services more than once. To do that they must be well satisfied. Why not make absolutely sure and **delight** them!

Time norm sheet

Activity or procedure	Estimated time taken now	Target average time
1.	....	....
2.	....	....
3.	....	....
4.	....	....
5.	....	....
6.	....	....
7.	....	....
8.	....	....
9.	....	....
10.	....	....
11.	....	....
12.	....	....

Remember that you are a leader as well as a manager. The more that you involve people in decisions which affect their working lives – be they **objectives** or **time norms** – the more committed they will be to implementing the agreed changes.

'Become time-obsessed. Virtually all staff processes can be shortened by between 50 per cent and 99 per cent. Directly tie performance evaluations to speed. Remember: "What gets measured gets done". Make speed pay.' TOM PETERS

Plan the day

The longest journey begins with a single step. You will never achieve an **objective** if you do not break it down into manageable steps. Each day should see you and your team some steps nearer to your projected and desired result.

Here it is necessary to remind you of only one key point: do not leave day planning to the last minute.

The case study of the disorganised manager

James Bright's train was late, so was the tube. He rushed into the office at 9.45 and gulped down the first of his many cups of coffee. 'Dammit Sue' he said to his secretary. 'I have left my pocket diary at home. What's on today?' He rummaged in his pocket for a bit of paper he had jotted some notes on, about what he wanted to do that day. 'Here is your desk diary', said his secretary helpfully, but with her usual sigh. 'Good, good, I can do my plan for the day now.' His secretary closed it. 'I'm afraid you can't', she said, 'the Chief Executive has been waiting to see you for 15 minutes.' 'Damn railways!'

Plan your day outline a week ahead and in detail on the eve of it.

The daily list

It is an essential discipline to compile a programme for the day. The daily plan is likely to take 15 minutes. In return for this investment you gain a sense of control, direction and freedom which is otherwise impossible.

Set time limits for all tasks. Get into the way of always estimating the amount of time required to do each job, such as conducting an interview or writing a report.

Then establish your priorities. A priority is composed of two elements in various mixtures: urgency and importance. Some people find it useful to have a system of letters, numbers or stars to make the various orders of priority. A letter system for example might include:

A Do it now, do it well

B Plan it in, spend quality time

C Do it quickly, doesn't require quality time

D Do later or in some cases delegate

If you have worked according to your sense of priorities you will have done the important jobs, and that is what managing your time is all about.

Urgency/importance matrix

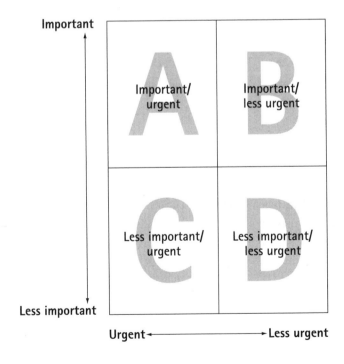

The daily plan

When to do it

Plan at the end of the previous day. This allows you to tidy up the loose ends and focus on tomorrow's priorities (allowing the subconscious to go to work on them).

OR

Alternatively you can plan at the beginning of the day, allowing you to focus on the day ahead, before getting involved with the details. This may also allow you to plan the day with and delegate work to your assistant and colleagues.

Choose which suits you best and ideally keep to it. Decide for yourself whether the beginning/end of the day happens at the work place or at home.

How to do it

List the components

a) Review yesterday's plan – what remains to be done – transfer to today's plan

b) Check the weekly plan – transfer items for completion into today's plan

c) Look at today's commitments and allocate time for preparation to complete efficiently

Prioritise the components

Put A, B or C against each component and a D for work to be delegated. Block together items such as phone calls, correspondence, etc.

Plan the day

Firmly decide when you will complete the one or two really important tasks of the day. Block some time out to deal with these just as you would a meeting. Consider when you will do the remaining tasks and tell your assistant about your plan.

Checklist – daily planning

If you find that your daily planning is not working very well, ask yourself first 'Am I at least achieving my highest priorities?' If the answer is 'No' or 'Doubtful' you should work through the following checklist.

1. Are you trying to accomplish too much in a day?

2. Did some tasks not get done because you were not ready at that time to do them?

3. Was the item or task clearly formulated?

4. Did you find it difficult to make decisions?

5. Did you have all the available information?

6. Had you neglected to plan sufficiently for the day because you were feeling under pressure?

7. Did you abandon the task because it was too difficult or too boring?

A review of this kind can establish whether or not your time budget was realistic in the first place. If it was, then the problem lies in the area of execution. The most common reason given to me by managers for failing to accomplish what they set out to achieve is summarised in one word – interruptions. To counter them, you must learn to use one of the shortest and most time saving words in the English language: 'NO'.

Learn to say no

It's no good talking about planning your day in order to achieve your objectives if your day is already full of meetings or activities that bear no relation to them at all. Why does this happen?

The reason is we find it hard to learn to say no, and so run up an enormous time-bill for ourselves, by the indiscriminate use of this plastic credit card:

But remember: be ruthless with time – gracious with people.

Key points

▶ Tactical planning focuses upon the immediate time available to you, which is measured out in days.

▶ Check your attitude to the present, for without concentrating on today, you will achieve nothing.

▶ Make out a list of what you want to do each day – mark them in order of priority. Do it the evening before, so that you can sleep on it.

▶ Review each day briefly, identify the successes and analyse the reasons for failures.

▶ Learn to say no, otherwise you will become merely the servant to the priorities of others.

▶ It is not easy to become efficient without becoming odious. Your practice of time management should enable you to contribute more to society and to others, not act as their judge.

'It's not enough to be busy. The question is: "What are you busy about?"' **HENRY THOREAU**

Make the best use
of your best time

A few minutes of reflection will tell you that the quality of your attention or concentration varies at different times. If you are very tired or suffering from jet lag, for example, the quality of your decisions will tend to degenerate. On the other hand, you may notice that you habitually tend to be more mentally alert, or at least more creative, at certain times of the day.

You may remember in this context the Pareto Principle? It states that 'The Significant items of a given group form a relatively small part of the Total'. For example, 20% of the buildings in London use up to 80% of the total electricity supplied to that city.

> **20% of your time produces 80% of your high-quality output.**

So, whatever else you do, make sure that you manage well that critical 20% of your time.

Checklist – do you make best use of your best time?

▶ Do you know clearly how much of a morning or night person you are?

▶ Do you regularly programme your day so that 'best time' is given to the highest grade activities, such as strategic thinking?

▶ Did you know that your manual dexterity – the speed and co-ordination with which you perform complicated tasks with your hands – peaks during the afternoon?

▶ Most of us seem to reach our peak of alertness around noon. Is that true of you?

► Did you know that your short-term memory is best in the morning – in fact, about 15% more efficient than at any other time of the day?

► As you tend to do best on cognitive tasks – things that require the juggling of words and figures in one's head – during the morning, do you pay special attention to planning your mornings?

► If it is your choice, when would you plan a meeting? The morning, the afternoon, or does it depend on what sort of meeting it is?

Organise office work

Time effectiveness in offices

Office literally means the place where much of the work is done. It may be the directing headquarters of an enterprise or organisation, or simply the place where a professional or self-employed person conducts professional business.

In this section we will concentrate on two key areas of this part of your time efficiency and effectiveness framework – organising paperwork and controlling interruptions.

How to control interruptions

An interruption is only an interruption if it is something that stops or hinders by breaking in on some continuity or other, such as writing a report or carrying out an interview.

Although most text books say that you should refuse to be interrupted (arrange to call back or fix a meeting), we all know in practice that it often makes sense to accept the interruption. But you must control it, otherwise it's goodbye to your 'To Do' list for that part of the day.

Dealing with interruptions

▶ Set a time limit and stick to it. Say 'I have five minutes – will that do or would you rather fix a time later?'

▶ Set the stage in advance: you are very busy with a deadline in sight.

▶ With casual droppers-in remain standing. If they sit down, perch on the edge of your desk.

▶ Arrange to meet in the other person's office if it is nearby – you can then determine when to leave.

▶ Avoid small talk when you are busy: it doubles interruption time.

- Get them to the point. Don't be afraid to interrupt the interrupter, asking them – what is the problem? What is the purpose of the call?

- Be ruthless with time but gracious with people. Give them your full attention. Listen well. Be firm but friendly and helpful. Do not let them go away empty-handed if you can avoid it.

- Have a clock available where visitors can see it, and don't be afraid to glance at it a few times. Explain about your next appointment, a white lie is better than a black interruption.

Checklist – paperwork

- Do you clear your desk of all papers except those relating to the particular job in hand?

- Is your work space so organised that the things you need are to hand?

- Do you really try to handle each piece of paper only once?

- Do you sort paperwork into categories in priority order?

- Have you eliminated unnecessary paperwork, and simplified the remainder where possible?

- Have you learnt to pick out quickly the key points or critical issue in letters and reports?

- Are you good at deciding what must be read through carefully and what can be skimmed?

- Have you developed a clear and succinct way of writing, so that you do not generate unnecessary paper for others?

- Have you developed techniques to manage interruptions – set a time limit, remain standing, have a clock in your office and use them appropriately?

- Do you use your secretary or assistant to screen potential interruptions?

Manage
meetings

Have you noticed that in some organisations managers seem to spend all their working time in meetings? They never seem to be available to talk to you – perhaps a potential customer or supplier.

Meetings, both of groups and between individuals, are obviously essential. You cannot lead or manage without them.

But, putting on your time management hat, you should constantly ask yourself three fundamental questions:

▶ Is this meeting really necessary?

▶ If so, how much of my time is the subject of it really worth?

▶ Will it begin on time and end on time?

There are various sorts of meetings – briefing, advisory, council, committee, negotiating. They can be divided into categories, roughly according to how decisions are taken. It is important to know what kind of meeting it is, but remember that a particular meeting may blend two or more of these basic types.

The effective board

From a recent survey of 500 directors, two-thirds of whom held the job titles of Chairman and/or Chief Executive, some 75% believed that the effectiveness of their companies' boards could be improved. Only one in eight of the companies questioned operated any form of periodic formal appraisal of personal effectiveness in the boardroom.

The cost of meetings

To reinforce your resolve to plan your meetings, it is worth developing a sense of the financial cost of meetings. The following chart gives you a picture of the cost of a person's time in ratio to their salaries.

Salary/ annum	5 Mins	15 mins	1 hour	1 day
£45,000	£2.25	£6.75	£27.00	£189.00
£40,000	£2.00	£6.00	£24.00	£168.00
£35,000	£1.75	£5.25	£21.00	£147.00
£30,000	£1.50	£4.50	£18.00	£126.00
£25,000	£1.25	£3.75	£15.00	£105.00
£20,000	£1.00	£3.00	£12.00	£84.00

The above figures are based on a working year of 238 days with one working day equal to seven hours. Overheads are not included. The chart highlights how costly time wasting can be at various salary levels.

Begin on time and end on time!

Meetings that both begin and end on time and complete their business, require both excellent presidents (and chairmen or women) and excellent team members.

The presiding person should have planned the meeting, establishing clearly the objective and the programme (or agenda) for achieving them, with more-or-less accurate estimates of the time needed for each of them. Then he or she has to communicate them to those at the meeting in such a way that everyone is committed to achieving the common objective. Thus a meeting needs both leading and managing if it is to be successful. Yet the leader has only 50% of the cards: successful outcome depends as much upon the quality of the contributions of the others involved.

With the shared policy of beginning and ending on time in mind, **self-discipline** is essential. The leader or chairman should set an example by talking less than other group members. When you are talking, be concise – remember the salary meter ticking if ten managers are listening to you being long-winded.

No substitute

The CEO of a large and well-known corporation posted the following inspiring slogans in his conference room:

'Intelligence is no substitute for information.'

'Enthusiasm is no substitute for capacity.'

'Willingness is no substitute for experience.'

One day the slogans were taken down, after somebody had scribbled underneath: 'A meeting is no substitute for progress.'

Points to ponder

It is useful to reflect from time to time about the meetings in our working lives, because they are both so essential and yet potentially so time-consuming.

The Greeks thought of it first?

Most people know that Socrates was put on trial for his life and died by drinking hemlock. How long do you think his trial lasted? Three months? Three weeks? No, it lasted just one day. For in Athens all trials were confined to one day. To make it work each speaker was confined to six minutes. Recently recovered from the ground in Athens have been the pottery water-clocks that determined the length of these speakers in the courts – six minutes each way.

Checklist – how effective are you as a manager of meetings?

▶ Do you keep the objectives of meetings clearly in mind?

▶ Are your meetings planned ahead? Do you decide who is to be present and circulate the agenda and any relevant information in advance?

▶ Do you agree time limits in advance, and start on time?

▶ Do you budget specific amounts of time for each item on the agenda? Do you include time to establish the aims of the meeting, to ensure effective discussion, to reach conclusions, and to agree the actions necessary?

▶ Do you make sure that minutes (if they are necessary) are concise and definite as to who is to do what, and by when?

▶ Do your meetings end on a positive note, with a summary of decisions taken and action to be implemented?

▶ Are you invariably successful when presiding over a meeting, at combining the two roles of referee and umpire?

▶ Have you developed a way of regularly appraising your performance as a chairman and eliciting feedback so that you can improve your skills?

▶ Do you review regular meetings to ensure that they are necessary and that the right people attend?

Delegate
effectively

Every position or role in an organisation has – or should have – defined responsibilities or functions, together with the authority to carry them out. Leading managers tend to have responsibilities for more work than they can possibly execute themselves. They need to delegate some of it to others, together with some of their own positional authority.

The benefit of effective delegation is that it gives you more time to lead and manage, especially where the following are involved:

▶ Complex and difficult management tasks

▶ Novel business developments

▶ Strategic opportunities

▶ Productivity and quality improvement

▶ Communication of vision and strategy

▶ Key staff appointments

▶ Staff development and training

▶ Spearheading marketing drives

▶ Staying close to major customers

▶ Getting out of the office and listening to people.

Decide what to delegate

If you are in a position requiring strategic or operational leadership, and you are coming under severe time pressures, you should delegate. Some types of work you should consider delegating are listed below:

▶ Repetitive routines of an administrative nature; minor decisions

▶ Technical or functional speciality activities as opposed to leading/managing functions

- ▶ Projects or tasks for which you are less qualified than some of your staff

- ▶ Work that will provide growth opportunities for employees

- ▶ Assignments that will give variety to routine work, or add to job satisfaction, or will increase the general pool of useful experience.

Skills of delegation

Selecting the right staff

It is no excuse to blame failure on the quality of your staff. You chose or accepted them. If they are too incompetent or unwilling to do the job, even with training, you should get rid of them.

Training and developing the individual

However high the potential of your staff – those to whom you wish to delegate – they will need training. Remember the training cycle:

- ▶ Demonstrate job with delegate alongside

- ▶ Get feedback and comment from him or her

- ▶ Get delegate to do job and observe

- ▶ Delegate does job on own and delegator is available to answer questions

- ▶ Delegate does job and reports back on completion.

Start with small routine tasks and build up to challenging tasks as confidence on both sides grows.

Briefing and checking understanding

Both the training process and subsequent delegation require considerable two-way communication skills on both parts. What is being delegated must be clearly defined; the authority to do it must be spelt out. Others involved also need to be informed. Check understanding. Make sure the person knows the wider context: company aims and policies. Then they will know why and how it has to be done.

Standing back and supporting

Resist temptations to get involved. Do not rush in and countermand a subordinate's orders. If they come to you, try not to provide the answers but help them to find them. Your aim is to develop the initiative of the subordinate, then they can cope with problems, including those caused by their actions, as well as you have done in the past.

Controlling in a sensible and sensitive way

No one likes to feel that there is no rope connecting them to the anchor. Check progress at agreed points. Remember always that abdication is not the name of the game. Control is the essence of delegation.

Checklist – are you a good delegator yet?

Remember that the most common complaint of subordinates is that their superiors will not delegate. How do you rate as a delegator?

▶ Are there areas of your work that you should be delegating, but for some reason or other you are not ready to do so?

▶ Do you work for more than nine hours a day?

▶ Do you take home work at weekends?

- ► When you delegate, do you clearly define the tasks you are delegating and make sure that the person who is carrying them out knows exactly what is expected of them?

- ► Do you, if you are honest with yourself, find it difficult to trust others to carry out some work for which you are accountable?

- ► Do you sometimes forget to delegate the necessary authority along with the delegated task?

- ► 'A delegated responsibility will always be carried out less well than I would have done it myself'. Do you agree?

- ► When delegating – do you seldom, if ever, engage people in the decision-making, problem-solving or creative thinking processes involved?

If you score seven or eight 'no' answers you are well on the way to becoming an excellent delegator.

Make use of committed time

You may sometimes complain that you lack time. But you have all the time there is for you.

Time comes in different guises. Basically, at work there is discretionary time – the time which you can choose to spend as you will – and committed time. Committed time is time that is booked for one reason or another. However, if you are alert you may find portions of it which are actually free time. Waiting in a bus queue is a good example, you are committed to be standing there, but you need not waste the time.

Exercise

Think of an example of committed time in the last week or two where you found unexpectedly that you had at least half an hour to spare.

- What did you do with it?
- Could you have put that time to better use?
- What would you need to have had with you in order to do so?

Some examples of committed time

Daily routines are in effect committed time. Take shaving for example. Nine out of ten men shave daily. Today, as in more primitive times, men devote more time to shaving than any other area of personal care. It is estimated that modern man spends 3,350 hours (that's 19 weeks) of his life standing in front of a mirror, scraping a layer of skin off his face, together with the growth of the previous day.

You may want to forget about the exercise bicycle, but have you considered using a tape recorder to learn or perfect a foreign language?

Take eating. Between the ages of 20 and 50 you will spend an estimated 8,000 hours eating – the equivalent of 330 days and nights. Notice however that we do use these committed times for social or business conversations.

Travel time

A major candidate for review is the time you spend travelling. It usually involves waiting time: both can be put to profitable use – thinking, reading, writing, conducting business meetings, or using a portable telephone. These activities are considerably more difficult, if not impossible, if you insist always on driving by car to wherever you need to go.

It's healthier and more time efficient by rail

A consultant neurologist wrote a letter to the The Times in 1991 in which he made the following points:

'Amongst the patients I see, yearly mileages of up to 60,000 are not uncommon. I have recently seen one patient who claims to be driving in excess of 100,000 miles per year. One patient told me that he spends seven hours in his car each day, and about 1 1/2 hours actually working. His wife, who works locally, does the opposite.

Many of the patients I see are salesmen and regional managers. Some need to carry heavy equipment or samples. Others visit clients in rural areas. For them, a car is probably a necessity. Others, however, travel from one city to another via the motorway. Most will readily admit that they only travel by car because the firm supplies the vehicle and pays the running costs'.

Does that make good time management sense to you?

Remember that a day has a hundred pockets of time if you know where to look for them.

Manage your health

> **Time management is about the quality of your time as well as the quantity.**

If you're not around in five years, your business is going to suffer. Even a few weeks off being avoidably ill is going to involve you in a major waste of productive time. Depending on the nature of your illness, of course, you may be able to claw back some of this involuntarily committed time – committed to your hospital bed – using it in some constructive way.

To give to your work and to others *high quality time* you must top up your energy levels. We all have to write cheques on our energy. But are you overdrawn? Do you make a practice of paying back the bank – your body, mind and spirit?

Checklist – do you really manage your energy levels?

Please think about each question honestly. Ask your spouse or a good friend to verify your answers.

1. Do you get enough sleep? The norm is eight hours, slightly less as you grow older. You can function on much less, but your creativity is 15% down.

2. Do you apply common sense to diet? There is a broad consensus on what is good for us to eat and drink. The golden rule is moderation in all things.

3. Do you take exercise? What kind of exercise you take and when is a personal matter, but are you really taking sufficient exercise?

4. Do you take holidays? 'Don't spare; don't drudge', said Benjamin Jowett. Remember that you can do a full year's work in 11 months but you cannot do it in 12 months. Do you take and enjoy full holiday time?

5. Do you allow time for reflection? It is a good idea to spend some time just meditating in a relaxed way about what you are doing in your work at present, even if it's only for a few minutes each day.

Coping with stress

Stress is caused by a number of factors. Some of them are outside our control. Some of them are the results of our own decisions – or indecision.

Are you – or any of your colleagues or subordinates – suffering from stress? The warning symptoms include:

*   Constant tiredness
*   Incessant worry
*   Increased use of alcohol
*   Excessive smoking
*   Over-eating
*   Reliance on sleeping pills
*   Drugs
*   Irritability
*   Lack of appetite
*   Indecisiveness
*   Forgetfulness
*   Erratic driving
*   Loss of humour
*   Nausea

- Fainting spells
- Tendency to sweat for no obvious reason
- Sleeplessness
- Nail-biting
- Nervous 'tics'
- Frequent crying or desire to cry
- Headaches and tension
- Frequent indigestion
- Loss of concentration
- Inability to relax
- Feeling unable to cope

Exercise

If you – or one of your team – begins to suffer from these symptoms, what action would you take?

Eliminate stress caused by poor time management

Sensible time management tackles most of the twelve most common roots of management stress. Research on 1000 managers in ten countries has identified these as follows:

☐ Time pressures and deadlines

☐ Work overload

☐ Inadequately trained subordinates

☐ Long working hours

☐ Attending meetings

☐ Demands of work on private and social life

☐ Keeping up with new technology

☐ Holding beliefs conflicting with those of the organisation

☐ Taking work home

☐ Lack of power and influence

☐ The amount of travel required by work

☐ Doing a job below one's level of competence

Please put a number in each box, listing your **stress potency quotient** (SPQ) from one (extremely high) to five (virtually non-existent).

Add up your score

12-24 You are already stressed. Take a day off, see your Doctor and **check your time management skills**!

25-44 You need to improve your time management across a wide front. Do not procrastinate.

45-59 Select particular areas for improvement and work on them without delay.

60 Fine, but how about the people working for you?

A final word

Time management should be **fun**. It doesn't have to be a complicated daily chore. Keep it as simple as possible.

The good news is that you will never meet the perfect time manager. We all fall short. You are probably already very good at managing your time; in some respects, however, you realise that you now could be better.

Why not make an appointment with yourself now in your year planner in about three months time, for a review of how you are getting on?

The wonderful thing is that tomorrow's 24 hours now await you – untouched and unwasted. You are now in a position to make more effective use of your time.

The end result of organising or managing your self and time properly is that you should be in good order. The end result of being in good order is that you are able to spend your energies, talents and time most effectively on the things that matter to you, and to start linking your daily planning to longer-term goals and objectives.

The second part of this book suggests some ways in which this can be achieved.

two

Personal development

Aims and objectives

The aim of this part of the book is to help you to:

- **Recognise and value past and present achievements**

- **Identify transferable skills and personal competence**

- **Clarify personal and professional goals**

- **Assess strengths and weaknesses in your range of competences**

- **Collect evidence for a portfolio of achievements**

- **Form clear development objectives**

- **Set up a development action plan**

- **Collect together evidence and information for a personal profile.**

There is no 'end' to the self-development process. By the time you have worked through the following sections, you will have a framework for ongoing development.

When you have customised it to your own needs, the framework for continuous improvement will help you to:

1. Improve performance in your present job

2. Develop appropriate skills and competences

3. Realise your full potential.

You can use it in a variety of situations, including:

- Your own self-development needs

- Appraisal sessions with line management

- Development planning sessions

- Internal and external interviews

- Planning a change of direction within your organisation

- Planning your personal career progression.

Overview

1. Where you are now

This section helps you to identify your current personal transferable skills and competences by assessing your present position and your past experience.

It also helps you to identify your strengths and weaknesses and provides an overview of your development.

2. How you can learn and develop

This section gives you information on how people learn. The material is based on Peter Honey and Alan Mumford's work on the learning cycle and individual learning styles. There is an exercise to help you assess your own learning preferences so that you can maximise your style.

3. Where you want to be

This section helps you to set objectives and any additional information you wish to include. You will be taken through a step-by-step process of setting and clarifying one objective. You can then record it and repeat the process for other objectives.

You will then be asked to turn your objective into an action plan. Guidelines on making achievable action plans are given.

4. Evaluate, check, review and update

This section is about reviewing, checking and updating the material you have collected about yourself, the objectives and the action plans you have set. Having achieved – or not achieved – your objectives and carried out your action plans, you will need either to review the original ones or go back to your overview of development goals and start the process again.

5. Your personal profile

In this section, you can summarise all the information you have gathered about yourself and create a personal profile. Guidance, suggestions and checklists on style, sequence and presentation are provided.

There are also basic guidelines for collecting evidence of your skills and competence: what to collect and what kind of things you can use. The guidelines are very brief and will only give you ideas on the kind of evidence you might need to accompany your personal profile.

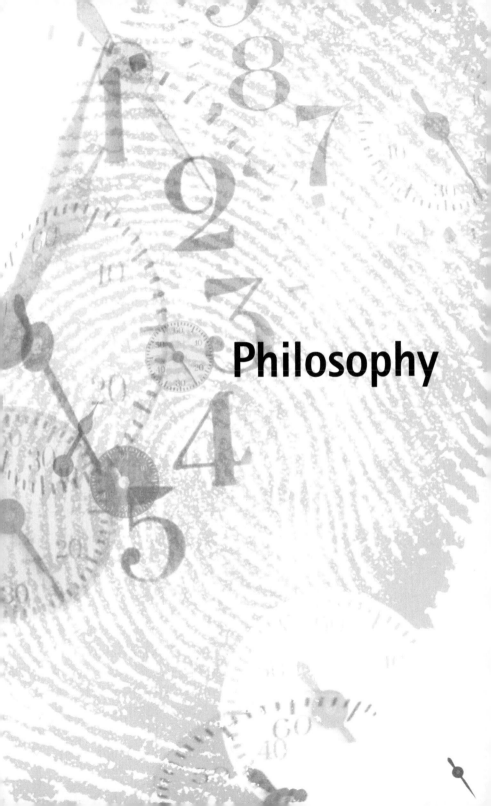

Philosophy

'The most successful nations in the future will be those which develop high quality, skilled and motivated workforces and make good use of them.'

1994 GOVERNMENT WHITE PAPER:
'COMPETITIVENESS: HELPING BUSINESS TO WIN'

A manager's role has changed in the last few years. The government, through the development of National Training Targets, Investors in People and the Vocational Qualification system (NVQs), is at the forefront of the drive towards lifetime learning, flexible self-development, continuous improvement and competence or core skills based training, linked directly to business goals.

The 'delayering', 're-engineering' and redundancy programmes following the recession of the '80's, encouraged companies to look for practical ways of helping their remaining 'empowered' employees to develop skills and knowledge for themselves. Individual managers became aware of the need to cope with the growing demand for flexibility. Whether self-development is part of a company initiative or something you are doing independently, this book will give you the tools to identify your competence, set objectives and make action plans for development – and keep the process going.

'The nineties will be a decade in a hurry' commented David Vice, an ex-Northern Telecom executive in 1993. *'There'll be only two kinds of manager, the quick and the dead.'* He was right: managers need to be proactive, flexible and willing to take more responsibility.

Looking to the future, the Institute of Management's report, *Management Development to the Millennium,* suggests that individuals are beginning to feel more positive about taking control of their working lives. Nearly 90% of those surveyed believed that they needed to increase their range of skills in the years to come. They realised that transferable skills are the key to improved prospects: a range of personal competences that they can transport to any job.

Developing personal competences – knowledge and skills that are transferable to a variety of situations – is part of the new manager's responsibility. Organisations are willing to provide the opportunities and resources for individuals to develop themselves – as long as individuals take those opportunities.

This book enables you to do just that. Here you have a starting point. It will not offer you the training nor the specialised competence checks you may need for your particular job. It will give you a framework for self-development.

A model of integrated management

Your responsibilities as a manager lie in three areas:

To the organisation

You have a responsibility to your organisation to help achieve business goals and realise the vision. The Management Charter Initiative (MCi), the lead body for national management standards, defines a manager's key purpose or task as: 'to achieve the organisation's objectives and continuously improve its performance'.

To the team

One of the major challenges facing managers in the next century will be dealing with the impact of flatter organisations where responsibility is devolved right across the workforce. Individual empowerment and team working, predicted in the '70's by management gurus, are finally becoming a reality. Managers are no longer 'bosses' but leaders of project-focused teams who must earn the respect of their team members. You have a responsibility to your team, to lead, support, develop and motivate them to realise the organisation's goals together with team goals and individual goals.

To your own individual development

You also have a responsibility to yourself – to develop your potential to the full. Using this book, you can develop your personal competences while working towards the model of integrated management.

The three areas are distinct but interconnected, as you can see. You will also note how they merge to form a conceptual model of integrated management. The model represents an amalgamation of the three circles model of leadership, described in Part 1, the MCi's personal competence model and the conviction that self-development is central to a manager's progression.

A model of integrated management

Key purpose of a manager

'To achieve the organisation's objectives and continuously improve its performance'

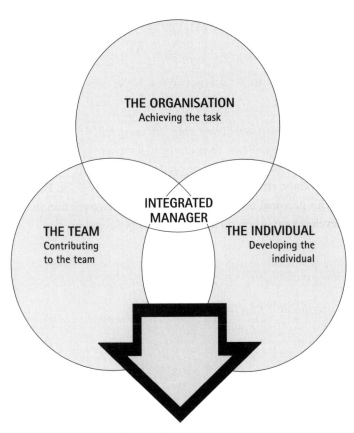

Personal competences

Showing concern for excellence
Setting and prioritising objectives
Monitoring and responding to actual against planned activities
Showing sensitivity to the needs of others
Relating to others
Obtaining the commitment of others
Presenting oneself positively to others
Showing self-confidence and personal drive
Managing personal emotions and stress
Managing personal learning and development
Collecting and organising information
Identifying and applying concepts
Taking decisions

The concept of competence

Competence is defined as: 'the ability of a manager to perform to the standards required in employment'.

Personal competence is regarded as the foundation of personal effectiveness and flexible management. To be able to perform effectively, managers need to bring a level of personal competence to their jobs. Personal competences are transferable and reflect the skills needed for the *process* of management: *how* things are done in order to be effective.

What needs to be done: the particular activities that are carried out are represented by key roles in the national management standards model and headings for the core competences in many organisations. They are:

- Managing operations
- Managing finance
- Managing people
- Managing information

The key roles are broken down into specific units of competence. These key role headings or 'areas' stay the same while the units of competence vary in range and scope with each level of management. The Model of Personal Competence, on the other hand, is the same for all levels of management and underpins the key roles at all levels.

The focus of this book is on developing personal competence: increasing your personal effectiveness in any management role so as to be able to deal with a variety of situations and jobs.

The Personal Competence Model

Clusters of personal competence	Dimensions of personal competence
1. Planning to optimise the achievement of results	1.1 Showing concern for excellence 1.2 Setting and prioritising objectives 1.3 Monitoring and responding to actual against planned activities
2. Managing others to optimise results	2.1 Showing sensitivity to the needs of others 2.2 Relating to others 2.3 Obtaining the commitment of others 2.4 Presenting oneself positively to others
3. Managing oneself to optimise results	3.1 Showing self-confidence and personal drive 3.2 Managing personal emotions and stress 3.3 Managing personal learning and development

continued over

4. Using intellect to optimise results	4.1 Collecting and organising information
	4.2 Identifying and applying concepts
	4.3 Taking decisions

Self-assessment

Self-assessment is recognised as valid both nationally and internationally. Research shows that it is as accurate and reliable as any assessment method. People do not upgrade themselves or give themselves 'extra points' as a rule – the most common criticism. Far from it – British people in particular have been shown to underestimate their abilities and to err on the side of caution. If you want the exercises to work, then be honest and don't be too hard on yourself!

Checking your perceptions

The last section in this guide invites you to check your assessment of yourself with someone else. It may be that you are using this book to prepare for an appraisal session or a development planning session with your manager, in which case your manager will provide the check. If not, then ask a colleague or your line manager to give you a few minutes to check their perceptions of you with your own. Better than that, complete the exercises at the same time as someone else, so that you can check each other's perceptions, discuss progress and keep each other on track.

Continuous improvement and self-development

However you decide to use this book, you will have started a cycle of ongoing development with built in quality evaluation and review elements. Once you have reviewed and evaluated your development progress, you begin again by updating your development objectives and action plan. That takes you back to the top of the continuous improvement cycle, where you start again. The following diagram illustrates the process.

The cycle of continuous improvement

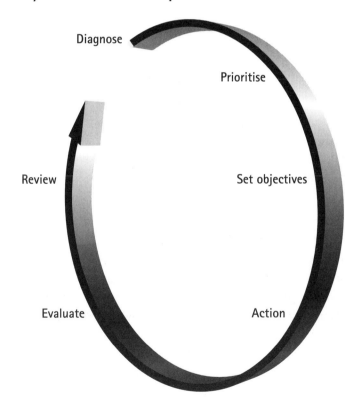

Diagnose

Prioritise

Review

Set objectives

Evaluate

Action

Being proactive and helping yourself

Before you start, think of the ways in which you can help yourself to take charge of your development. Jot down at least four proactive things you can do.

1..

....

2..

....

3..

....

4..

....

This book will help you on your way to professional development. You can use it in isolation, but to make it work you must be proactive and ask for the help, support and resources you need.

Some suggestions for being proactive:

1. Ask your manager for a development planning session

2. Set yourself clear development objectives

3. Create a realistic development plan for yourself

4. Find out what resources for training there are in your company

5. Find out what is available outside the company and ask for appropriate training

6. Ask for help and support and evaluate and review your progress regularly.

Checklist – key personal competences

Complete the following checklist for a general overview of your personal competence profile. It will not be definitive, as you will refine or even change it as you work through this package. It is the beginning of the process of identifying your strengths and weaknesses. Key personal competences appear in bold type above each group of questions.

Completing the key personal competences checklist

Circle **yes** or **no** under each of the dimensions of personal competence overleaf, according to your answer to the questions.

Try to be definite about your answers – if you are not sure of the answer, then circle **no**. It may make you look less competent than you actually are, but you will have a better idea of where your strengths and weaknesses lie. If you cannot answer with a **yes** or a **no**, then leave it without an answer – this still means that you need to work on it. You will be looking in more detail at your areas of skill and competence in the next section, and you can compare your findings and refine your answers.

There are 46 questions to think about and answer. You may want to break the activity up into bite-sized chunks and complete it in between other tasks.

Alternatively, go through it very quickly first, answering the 'easy' questions and return to the others at another time

Showing concern for excellence

Do you:

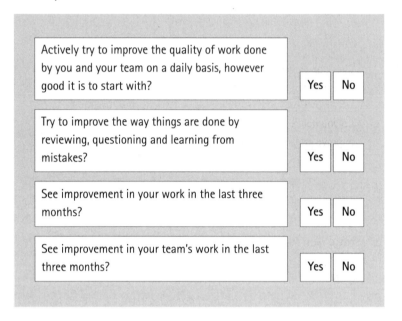

Actively try to improve the quality of work done by you and your team on a daily basis, however good it is to start with? | Yes | No

Try to improve the way things are done by reviewing, questioning and learning from mistakes? | Yes | No

See improvement in your work in the last three months? | Yes | No

See improvement in your team's work in the last three months? | Yes | No

Setting and prioritising objectives

Do you:

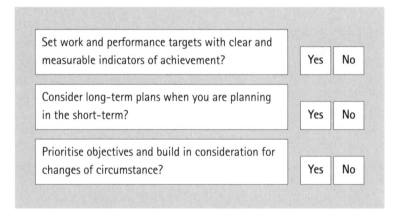

Set work and performance targets with clear and measurable indicators of achievement? | Yes | No

Consider long-term plans when you are planning in the short-term? | Yes | No

Prioritise objectives and build in consideration for changes of circumstance? | Yes | No

Monitoring and responding to actual against planned activities

Do you:

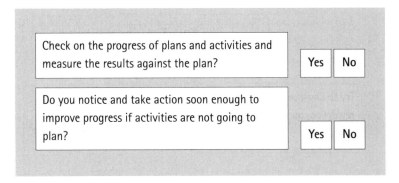

Check on the progress of plans and activities and measure the results against the plan? Yes No

Do you notice and take action soon enough to improve progress if activities are not going to plan? Yes No

Showing sensitivity to the needs of others

Do you:

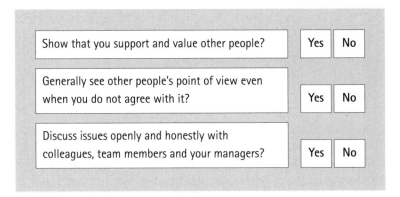

Show that you support and value other people? Yes No

Generally see other people's point of view even when you do not agree with it? Yes No

Discuss issues openly and honestly with colleagues, team members and your managers? Yes No

Relating to others

Do you:

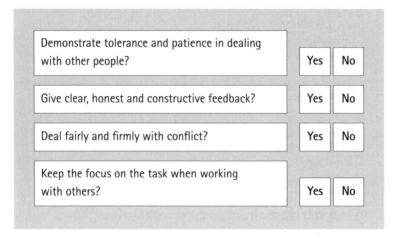

Demonstrate tolerance and patience in dealing with other people?	Yes	No
Give clear, honest and constructive feedback?	Yes	No
Deal fairly and firmly with conflict?	Yes	No
Keep the focus on the task when working with others?	Yes	No

Obtaining the commitment of others

Do you:

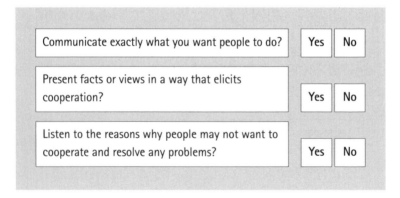

Communicate exactly what you want people to do?	Yes	No
Present facts or views in a way that elicits cooperation?	Yes	No
Listen to the reasons why people may not want to cooperate and resolve any problems?	Yes	No

Presenting oneself positively to others

Do you:

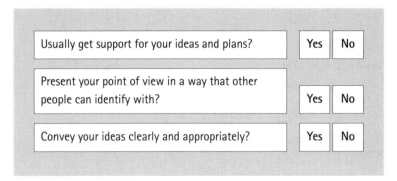

Usually get support for your ideas and plans?	Yes	No
Present your point of view in a way that other people can identify with?	Yes	No
Convey your ideas clearly and appropriately?	Yes	No

Showing self-confidence and personal drive

Do you:

Know what you want and where you're going?	Yes	No
Maintain commitment and determination despite setbacks?	Yes	No
Generally take control of events and situations?	Yes	No
Take responsibility for the consequences of your behaviour or actions?	Yes	No

Managing personal emotions and stress

Do you:

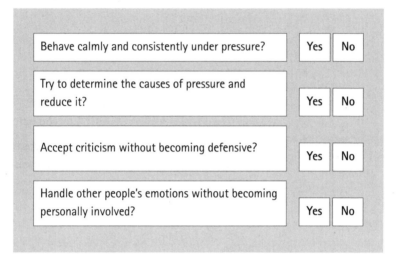

Behave calmly and consistently under pressure?	Yes No
Try to determine the causes of pressure and reduce it?	Yes No
Accept criticism without becoming defensive?	Yes No
Handle other people's emotions without becoming personally involved?	Yes No

Managing personal learning and development

Do you:

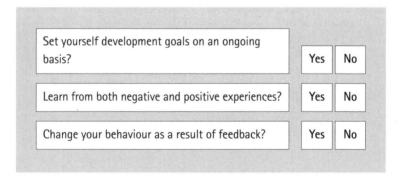

Set yourself development goals on an ongoing basis?	Yes No
Learn from both negative and positive experiences?	Yes No
Change your behaviour as a result of feedback?	Yes No

Collecting and organising information

Do you:

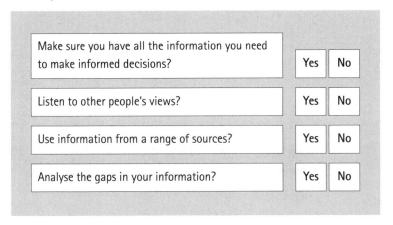

Make sure you have all the information you need to make informed decisions?	Yes / No
Listen to other people's views?	Yes / No
Use information from a range of sources?	Yes / No
Analyse the gaps in your information?	Yes / No

Identifying and applying concepts

Do you:

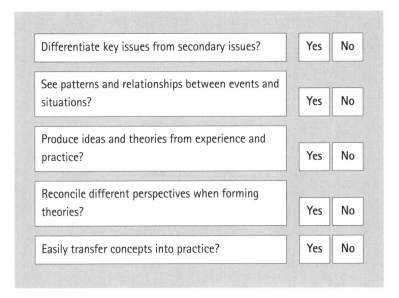

Differentiate key issues from secondary issues?	Yes / No
See patterns and relationships between events and situations?	Yes / No
Produce ideas and theories from experience and practice?	Yes / No
Reconcile different perspectives when forming theories?	Yes / No
Easily transfer concepts into practice?	Yes / No

Taking decisions

Do you:

Make decisions rather than just 'let things happen'?	Yes	No
Make decisions that are consistent?	Yes	No
See a variety of solutions before deciding?	Yes	No
Balance logic with intuition when deciding?	Yes	No
Think about where you want to be and what you want to be doing?	Yes	No

Competence check

Look at the number of **yes** answers you gave. Jot down the dimensions (in bold type) where you gave all **yes** answers. These are your strongest dimensions.

Now look at your **no** answers. If there were any dimensions where you answered **no** to all the questions, write them down at the top of your list. These are obviously your weakest dimensions. Rank the rest according to the ratio of **no** answers to the number of questions under each dimension heading.

Now you know where to start! Have a break and start again with the next section.

Where you
are now

'The abilities employers demand currently are often referred to as personal transferable skills, which include communication, numeracy, leadership, decision making and teamworking.'

GRAHAM WADE, THE GUARDIAN BUSINESS
MANAGEMENT, JANUARY 1996

Before you start on your programme of self-development, you need to have a clear idea of where your starting point is. The first exercise in this section is about identifying and documenting your past achievements. Then you will have the background to the picture you are building up of yourself. Of course, you will already know about it, but you can start analysing it in terms of what it says about you: the skills and knowledge demonstrated. As a bonus, you could be pleasantly surprised at how good you look on paper when you see all the data together. You will be using the information later, when you develop your personal profile.

In the previous section, you were introduced to the concept of personal competence: the fundamental skills that contribute to the process of management: *how* a job is done rather than what is done. These skills are transferable to any management position and are also known as personal transferable skills.

The second exercise in this section concentrates on the transferable skills and competence you have, by asking you to log current activities, identify the skills you are using daily and map your personal competence. In the process, you will also be able to identify competence gaps so that you can address them in the next section.

Exercise 1: Logging your achievements

It is not easy to conjure up a list of past achievements from thin air. You need to find a way of categorising them. A few categories are provided below to help you make your list, but don't be hidebound by these, you may think of other categories. Use the 'miscellaneous' space at the end of the page or start on a new sheet.

Leave the right hand columns blank for now: you will be using them later. You will also be asked to use this list when collecting information for your personal profile, so make it readable! Also, don't forget achievements and awards outside work: they demonstrate personal competence, too.

Jot down anything you can think of, however unlikely it may seem (a bronze medal in drama may seem weak until you use it to show your ability to present yourself, for example) – you can weed out the irrelevant ones later.

Achievements

Educational qualifications

....

....

....

....

....

Professional qualifications

....

....

....

....

....

Skill/knowledge

....

....

....

....

....

....

....

....

....

Achievements

Certificates

....

....

....

....

Skill/knowledge

....

....

....

....

Awards

....

....

....

....

....

....

....

....

Courses completed and/ or attended

....

....

....

....

....

....

....

....

....

....

Miscellaneous

....

....

....

....

....

....

....

....

Categories like 'awards' or 'qualifications' are easily defined. Not so easy are the achievements within your jobs or roles. These are just as important, so think hard about it. The 'results' are the outcomes of the achievements – why it was an achievement and what it achieved for the organisation, team or individuals involved. Once again, write down everything that occurs to you and weed out later.

Achievements in work

1. Achievement   Skill/knowledge

....

....

....

....

Result

....

....

....

2. Achievement

....

....

....

....

Result

....

....

....

Achievements in work

3. Achievement   Skill/knowledge

....

....

....

....

....

Result

....

....

....

4. Achievement

....

....

....

....

....

Result

....

....

....

Now have a break!

Read through all your achievements and use the right hand 'Skills' column to jot down:

▶ The practical, specialised or technical underlying skills demonstrated. (A brief list is provided as a guide – it is not exhaustive, but it will give you a idea of where to start)

▶ The knowledge demonstrated

▶ The dimensions of personal competence (listed overleaf) demonstrated.

Use your own shorthand if there is not enough space for the whole personal competence title. Obviously, some of the underlying skills will duplicate the competence. You can rationalise them later.

Don't worry about educational and other qualifications – it is obvious that Maths GCSE demonstrates a level of skill in maths, for example.

Underlying skills you could include:

▶ Keyboard skills

▶ Reading for facts

▶ Problem solving

▶ Reviewing, evaluating

▶ Developing ideas

▶ Budgeting

▶ Working in a team

▶ Speaking in public

▶ Physical tasks

▶ Using computer data

▶ Organising tasks

▶ Analysing information

- ▶ Seeing alternatives
- ▶ Working creatively with space or words
- ▶ Checking detail
- ▶ Designing events
- ▶ Initiating change

Dimensions of personal competence

- ▶ Showing concern for excellence
- ▶ Setting and prioritising objectives
- ▶ Monitoring and responding to actual against planned activities
- ▶ Showing sensitivity to the needs of others
- ▶ Relating to others
- ▶ Obtaining the commitment of others
- ▶ Presenting oneself positively to others
- ▶ Showing self-confidence and personal drive
- ▶ Managing personal emotions and stress
- ▶ Managing personal learning and development
- ▶ Collecting and organising information
- ▶ Identifying and applying concepts
- ▶ Taking decisions

Competence check

Look through the skills, knowledge and competence in the right hand column on page 94 and make a note under the following headings of the underlying skills and personal competences that appear most often. Rank order them according to how often they appear.

Skills and knowledge demonstrated

....

....

....

....

Personal competence demonstrated

....

....

....

....

This will give you an overview of the skills and competences that are most developed. Compare this competence check with the list of strongest and weakest competences from the introductory checklist. You may have concentrated on developing different skills in your current circumstances.

The achievements log

Now start rationalising your work achievements, thinking about the range of skills you can demonstrate, and checking that the achievements are no more than three to five years old. Think about two or three achievements. Record this information to give you the basis for an ongoing log.

Keep your achievements log up-to-date: add information as it happens.

Exercise 2: Personal competence and skills activity analysis

Write down one activity you have performed or have been involved in over the last few days. For example: a team meeting, project briefing, budgeting activity or a presentation. Choose a whole activity with a beginning and an end, like a meeting, rather than a small task.

Identify the skills involved in the course of that activity. It may surprise you to see how many personal skills you use at one time.

For example, in a team meeting you might seek to improve performance; encourage others to assess progress and effectiveness; identify problems; see others' point of view; maintain focus on task; demonstrate clear purpose; encourage exchange of information; differentiate key issues from irrelevant ones; and check own logic with others.

Competence evaluation

Now read through the skills you have logged for the activities and tick the ones where you are most competent. Put a cross against any skills you feel you need to develop.

When you have done that, draw up a priority list of skills from the ones that you crossed. Compare this list with your findings under the 'weaker' headings from the competence check in the introduction to Part 2. You can use this information when you clarify your development objectives in Section 3.

Summary

In this section you have gathered information about your achievements to date, and the skills you have. This provides you with background information about your competences. You can also use it when you put together your personal profile.

You have also identified some of the transferable skills you use currently and evaluated your competence in them. You will be using this information when you come to setting development objectives.

The next section is about how you can learn both formally and informally, the methods available, your preferences and what you can do to help yourself.

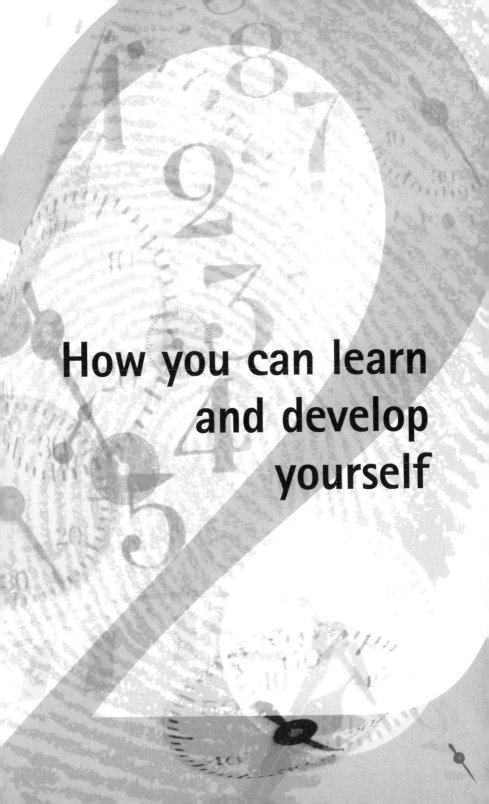

How you can learn and develop yourself

In this section, you will be looking at the learning cycle and the different ways that people learn. You will look briefly at the resources available to you, both inside and outside of your organisation, and examine ways of making your learning style more flexible.

The material in this section has been abbreviated and adapted from the work of Peter Honey and Alan Mumford.

The learning cycle

The process of learning can be broken down into four stages and represented as a cycle. The fourth step leads back into the first and creates a continuous process.

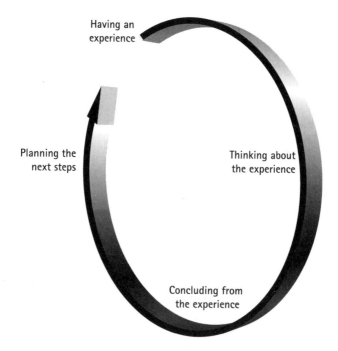

None of the stages are effective on their own. A person can have an experience and learn nothing from it, for example, or conclude from an experience and not use those conclusions in practice. A fully developed learner goes through each stage of the process in turn and arrives back at the first stage ready to start again. Knowledge acquired from one experience adds to the next experience and so on.

Learning stages/learning styles

Most people have a preference for particular stages of the process because of their personality style or the way they have developed – their learning style preferences. The learning styles are:

▶ Activist

▶ Reflector

▶ Theorist

▶ Pragmatist.

These styles fit into the learning cycle:

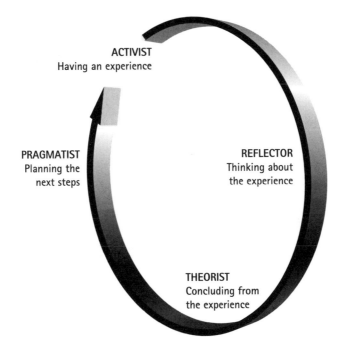

ACTIVIST
Having an experience

PRAGMATIST
Planning the
next steps

REFLECTOR
Thinking about
the experience

THEORIST
Concluding from
the experience

Having a strong preference for one style over another means that the learning process is incomplete. The next activity will help you to identify your own preferred styles. If you are aware of these and can understand where your weaker areas are, you can choose learning methods that will work for you or that will stretch you. You will also be able to understand other people's learning preferences, which helps if you are coaching, mentoring or training other people.

No learning style is better than any other. Having a learning style preference simply means that this is the way you tend to learn. There are advantages and disadvantages to each style, as you will see in the brief descriptions of each style given after the following questionnaire. Being aware of those advantages and disadvantages means that you can make allowances for your own style and understand other people's starting points.

The questionnaire

Put a tick against any of the questions, opposite, that you identify with, or a cross against any that you definitely do not identify with. You don't have to answer all of the questions in this way. If you feel that the question does not apply to you one way or the other, leave it blank. You should end up with a minimum of eight or ten responses.

Don't just think about learning situations. These questions are about general behaviour as well as learning behaviour.

Do you:

Time your work and plan everything logically, step by step?

Rarely feel enthusiastic about an idea until you are comfortable with it?

Act on impulse and plunge into things without thinking them through?

Think about the theory and systems behind the learning?

Prefer to work on your own?

Tend to listen to discussions or read about ideas first before jumping in with your views?

Plan and prioritise projects realistically?

Approach new ideas and challenges with enthusiasm, then get bored with them?

Research as many sources of information as possible before doing anything?

Put theory and ideas into practice?

Articulate your thoughts and talk things through with people?

Try to do things properly?

Revise and redraft your work often before you get to the finished product?

Achieve results through enthusiasm and quick thinking rather than through planning?

Pose the question: Does it work? or How does it work? in learning situations and at work?

Test, check and question your own and other people's ideas and work until you are sure that it is right?

Avoid detailed, methodical work and paperwork if at all possible?

Put your point straight away, without beating around the bush?

Really enjoy doing a job thoroughly and well?

Respect and listen to other people's ideas?

Scoring

The first letter in each of the questions indicates the learning style represented by that behaviour. For example, 'Avoid detailed, methodical work and paperwork if at all possible' indicates an Activist tendency and 'Respect and listen to other people's ideas' indicates a Reflector tendency.

▶ Questions beginning with A represent Activist behaviour

▶ Questions beginning with R represent Reflector behaviour

▶ Questions beginning with T represent Theorist behaviour

▶ Questions beginning with P represent Pragmatist behaviour

Write down the number of questions you ticked or crossed beginning with:

Ticks	**Crosses**
A	**A** ....
R	**R** ....
T	**T** ....
P	**P** ....

The highest number of ticks indicates your strongest learning style(s).

The highest number of crosses indicates your weakest style(s).

A brief description of each style

Activist

Activists love new experiences. They tend to be enthusiastic about new ventures and experiences, flexible and ready to adapt. They will ' have a go' and jump into an experience, without always thinking of the consequences. They tend not to plan, but go from one activity to the next, thinking on their feet. They sometimes find it hard to sit still and they tend to get bored easily. They might start a project with great enthusiasm and then lose interest when they have to concentrate on the planning and the detail. They are always the first to have their say in meetings and have ideas easily in 'brain-storming' situations. They tend to be outgoing and gregarious, if a little self-centred .

Reflector

Reflectors like to have time to think about things from all angles. They like to collect as much information as possible about a subject – from reading and listening to other people's views – before coming to conclusions. This often means that they take a long time coming to a conclusion. They like to put facts and information into perspective, and see the 'big picture'. In meetings they will be watching for the interactions of other people, as well as listening to ideas before they voice their own. They are thoughtful and wary of jumping into situations.

Theorist

Theorists like to conceptualise their theories and their learning. They like to feel that whatever they do is founded on a sound rationale. They think in a step-by-step logical way and can go off on theoretical tangents, leaving practicality behind. They like to analyse data and tidy it up, intellectually. They can be rigid and perfectionist and intolerant of emotional and subjective thinking. In meetings they tend to be quiet but attentive. If they have something to say, they will say it and stick to their guns through thick and thin. They can be irritated by flippancy and wary of unstructured situations.

Pragmatist

Pragmatists like to be practical, and ask the question 'How can I use this?' They want to get on with the action rather than listen to theory. They tend to be intolerant of 'airy fairy' ideas and always want to get to the point. They are open to new challenges and like to solve problems and make decisions. In the push for practicality, they can be too hasty and go for 'quick fixes' rather than exploring other avenues. They like to work under their own steam and at their own pace and get great satisfaction from making ideas work.

Developing your learning style

Keeping a learning log will help you to review your experiences, reach conclusions and plan what you can do better, using any experiences that you have. The activity of keeping a log like this makes you review your experiences and examine your learning with a view to improving it.

You can use any experience – it does not have to be a specific learning experience.

Creating a learning log

1. Choose an experience you have had recently at work. It could be a team session, writing a report or giving a presentation. Alternatively you could choose to focus on a specific learning experience – where you have been coached or been involved in a training event of some kind. Focus on one part of the experience – you don't have to write everything down.

2. Write a detailed account of what happened during that period of activity. Don't try to decide what you have learnt from it at this stage, just get the sequence of events down.

3. List the things you learnt or conclusions you reached after thinking about the experience. For example, in a meeting you could have learnt that you need to think your arguments through more thoroughly, as someone picked holes in your (good) idea and you were unable to defend it. If you are concentrating on a learning experience, think about the way you reacted. For example, you may have felt frustrated with someone coaching you as they were wasting time giving you background that you already knew, while you just wanted to know what to do.

4. Think hard about the learning points you have made. Think about how you could deal with the situation better next time or get more out of the experience. For example, in the coaching situation you may have learnt something from the background information if you had listened properly and asked questions rather than just feeling impatient. Make your plan as specific as possible, stating what you are going to do and when you will do it.

Ways of learning

The following list of learning activities is not exhaustive and includes only a few informal learning experiences. Add your own extra learning methods at the end of the list, with comments on the style(s) it may suit.

Training courses/workshops

These are the traditional training courses: away from the workplace, led by a trainer with a group of people brought together specifically for the training.

Best suits: Activists, Reflectors

Team training

These are training sessions involving a team working together often on a real-life project.

Best suits: Activists, Reflectors, Pragmatists

Self study

This method involves working alone with a workbook or a computer.

Best suits: Theorists, Reflectors, Pragmatists

Secondment

Secondment involves learning about something new by actually doing the job in another department, with people who do that job themselves.

Best suits: Activists, Pragmatists

Coaching

This means being shown how to do something then being guided through the stages as they occur and at the learner's own pace. The coach offers support and explanation, and takes responsibility for the training and the outcome.

Best suits: All styles

Action learning projects

This is a learning experience where a task or project is set up within the work situation, so that people can learn from doing it.

Best suits: Activists, Pragmatists

Networking

This is an informal way of learning and finding out about things. The network can include colleagues, people in different departments, external contacts, friends and family members. Many people in work use this method already by just asking people how to do things, or phoning a colleague or friend for information.

Best suits: All styles

Job rotation/multiskilling

This method involves moving people from one job to another, usually within a function. People move around from one part of the job to another to develop different skills and to promote teamwork.

Best suits: Activists, Theorists

Reading, watching television programmes or videos, listening to the radio

These are things that people do informally to increase their knowledge and find out about things. Some people do this consciously and plan their programmes, while others just follow their interests.

Best suits: Theorists, Reflectors

Mentoring

A mentor is there to help, advise and explain while learning – whether it is self study or on the job learning that is taking place.

Best suits: All styles

Action for learning

Find out about the availability of training within your organisation and the methods used. Ask your manager or training/personnel department about it and about how you can take advantage of the opportunities on offer. If the organisation is too small to have in-house training, find out about self-study courses, night classes and other events. Ring your local Training and Enterprise Council or a Further Education college. The opportunities are there if you want to take them.

Decide on the skills you want to develop and the methods available that would suit you. Give yourself a starting date – and begin.

Where you
want to be

Objective setting and action planning

People need goals: realistic, well targeted and challenging objective, in order to stay motivated. Working without them is like running a race blindfold. You need to set yourself goals and objectives at intervals during the self-development process so that you:

▶ Know what you are trying to achieve

▶ Know how well you are doing

▶ Know what to do in order to move on.

The journey of self-development does not follow a straight road – you could find yourself in a cul-de-sac because of a wrong turning or a badly targeted objective. Night classes in philosophy may seem appealing and could develop your intellect, but they won't help you with strategic management. Of course, you may want to do it as a leisure activity, but that is an entirely different matter.

Your development has to be focused and relevant for you to get anything out of it – not only so that you feel you are going somewhere but also because it acts as a demotivator if it doesn't work. A failed philosophy night class is worse than no night class at all!

Self-development is a lifelong process – so much has already been agreed. So how can you have goals? Surely the goal is self-development – and as it's an ongoing process – more self-development? – and then more? The answer is in setting long-term, medium-term and short-term goals: breaking the process up into bite-sized chunks.

This section will give you guidance on setting development objectives and making them happen.

Setting 'SMARTER' objectives

Self-development is a journey not a destination. You don't just get there and leave it at that – which is why your **SMART** objectives need to be even **SMARTER**:

▶ Specific

▶ Measurable

▶ Agreed

▶ Realistic

▶ Time-bound

▶ Evaluated

▶ Reviewed.

Long-term development goals

To start with, think about where you want to be, or what you want to be doing in ten years time (this can be lifestyle, work, another country, anything).

Now think about where you want to be and what you want to be doing in your work/career in three years time.

The first goal is a long-term goal, and can be wide ranging and blurred round the edges. The second is medium-term and more specific. You should already be thinking about the short-term 'stepping stone' objectives that will take you there. As they are shorter term, they need to be even more specific.

Your development objectives

Look through all the data you have gathered about yourself so far: the findings from the competence checklist and competence checks, the personal competence and transferable skills analysis and your learning plan.

Exercise: Clarifying objectives

For this exercise, choose one area you would like to develop. At the end of the process, you will have one objective. Then you can start on the next one.

The area I would like to develop is:

....

....

Draft your objective, stating clearly and specifically what you want to achieve.

For example, your area for development may have been 'team leadership'. Your draft objective could therefore be: 'To increase my effectiveness as a team leader.'

....

....

Now check that it meets the criteria for a **SMARTER** objective, asking the following questions and revising your draft, if necessary.

Make it SPECIFIC

Ask yourself:

- Does it say exactly what you want to do?
- Why do you want to achieve it?
- Is it specific enough?

For example, 'To increase effectiveness as a team leader' covers a number of areas. Your effectiveness may be hampered by your reluctance to deal with conflict. You would then rewrite your objective as: 'To increase my effectiveness in conflict situations.'

....

....

Make it MEASURABLE

Ask yourself:

- How will you know when you have reached the objective?
- What will have changed?
- How will other people react to you as a result of achieving your objective?

For example, 'I will stop avoiding conflict by giving in or supporting the wrong cause because it is easiest.'

....

....

Make it AGREED

Ask yourself:

Is there anyone I need to agree this objective with?

For example, your line manager or HR department, or anyone else you need support from.

....

....

Make it REALISTIC

Ask yourself:

Am I able to achieve this within the boundaries of my work schedule, my abilities and my other commitments?

Talk to a colleague or your manager about whether your objective is realistic.

Write down whom you need to agree it with.

....

....

Make it TIME-BOUND

Ask yourself:

When do I want to have achieved this by?

Set a realistic date for completion.

Make it EVALUATED AND REVIEWED

Ask yourself:

- When will I review the objective?
- Is it still workable?

Set a review date (this may be the same as the achievement date, or you can decide on an interim review date).

Make it STRATEGIC

Ask yourself:

Is your development objective aligned with organisational, operational and team goals and objectives?

Make it MEANINGFUL

Ask yourself:

Do you want to achieve this for yourself rather than because you feel it is expected of you?

Make it ATTAINABLE

Ask yourself:
Are there any barriers (external or internal) that may stop you from achieving this?

If so, how can you overcome them?

....

....

Make it REWARDING

Ask yourself:
- What will it do for you?
- Is it rewarding enough to keep you motivated and committed to it?

Make it TEAM-BUILDING

Ask yourself:
Will achieving this objective help me to contribute to my team?

Make it EMPOWERING

Ask yourself:
Will it make me feel more confident, in control and able to use my potential more effectively?

ACTION PLANNING

Your objective is a statement of intent. To make sure you achieve it, you need to plan a course of action. Using the objective you have just clarified, take the following steps to formulate an action plan.

1. **START NOW!** Decide what your first step will be. Once you have started, the others will follow.

    ....

    ....

2. Break up the plan into smaller tasks, and write them down in sequence. Be specific about what you will do.

    ....

    ....

3. Give yourself a completion date for each one.

4. Write down the resources or support you will need for each task.

5. Allow for changes to your plan. Review each task after it is completed.

Summary

In this section you have defined and clarified one development objective, making it:

- ▶ Specific
- ▶ Measurable
- ▶ Agreed
- ▶ Realistic
- ▶ Time-bound
- ▶ Evaluated and Reviewed
- ▶ Strategic
- ▶ Meaningful
- ▶ Attainable
- ▶ Rewarding
- ▶ Team-building
- ▶ Empowering.

You then use the following progression to make your objective into an action plan:

- ▶ Decide what you are going to do **today**
- ▶ Be specific about what you will do
- ▶ Write the smaller tasks in a logical flow
- ▶ Make dates for the achievement of each task
- ▶ Identify resources and support
- ▶ Allow for changes to your plan. Review after each task is completed
- ▶ Set dates for review.

The next section looks at the process of evaluation and review and checking your perceptions.

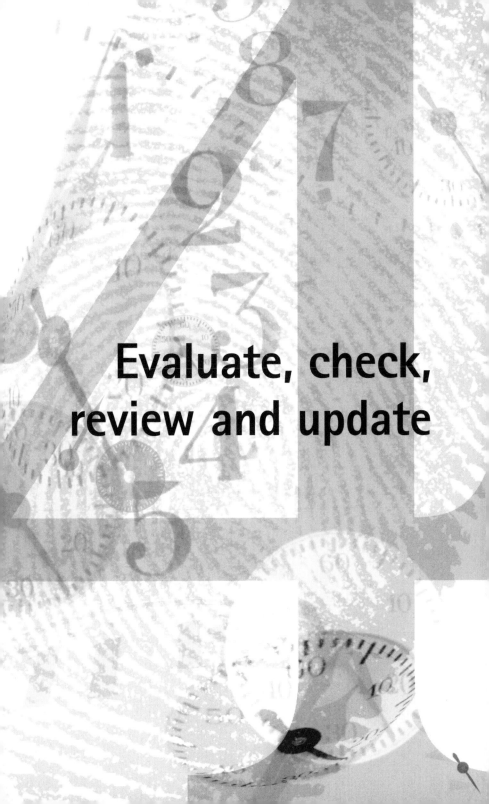

Evaluate, check, review and update

All the way through this guide, you have been asked to specify review dates and have been encouraged to make comments and be prepared to change. As this is an ongoing process, it is vital that you complete the learning cycle by evaluating, checking your perceptions, reviewing and updating your original objectives and amending action plans.

Progress checklist

It will have taken you some time to have worked your way through to this section, so you will have some idea of how your development is progressing. It is time to evaluate and review your progress so far:

▶ Have you set review dates?

▶ Have you transferred them to your diary?

▶ Have you evaluated the effectiveness of your objectives and plans?

▶ Have you reviewed them in the light of that evaluation?

▶ Have you changed anything?

▶ Has that made a difference to the way they are working out?

▶ Have you checked any of your perceptions with someone else?

▶ Have you updated any objectives, or set new ones yet?

If you answered **yes** to all the questions above, you are doing extremely well! If you answered **no** to all of them, you need to evaluate and review your commitment to the process, your methods or your time management skills.

Evaluate and review your progress

Setting objectives and just hoping that they will achieve themselves is not enough. Neither is thinking that you have 'more or less' kept to your plans. You have to track your performance and check that you are achieving objectives. If you are not, then you need to review them, think again about whether they are realistic or achievable, and update them.

If you are, then you can start on new challenges, with new objectives and with a success behind you.

When you have gone through all the lists and plans you have made so far: logging, reviewing and writing in your comments, write down any comments that occur to you and make suggestions for improvement and change.

Remember to:

▶ Keep your actions for change clear, short and achievable

▶ Only attempt one change at a time

▶ Make sure you are targeting the right component: changing an action plan will make no difference if your objectives are not realistic

▶ Start with the objective and analyse that before you look at your action plan.

Be proactive: ask for help and support

It can be very difficult to maintain motivation in isolation – particularly when things go wrong. It helps if you have made an arrangement – a contract with someone else who will support, encourage, make suggestions and remind you of your commitment. Make a formal appointment with that person to review progress at one, two or three month intervals. Make sure you both put them in your diaries and **keep the appointment**.

You also need a 'reality check' for your objectives and action plans. This is another good reason for asking someone to help.

What do other people think of you?

The reality check is vital in any review. You need to check your assumptions about yourself and to open your mind to the possibility of learning from their observations.

Everyone has a 'blind spot' about themselves, however self-aware they are, which often means that they don't see their strengths as well as their weaknesses. Talking your thoughts through with someone else may give you insights into your own personality and abilities, because you will be talking about yourself in an objective way. You have to ask for observations about yourself – other people don't often tell you the good things about yourself!

Giving feedback

If you are in the position of giving the feedback, these notes will be useful. Your task is to listen carefully and help the other person to talk through issues and clarify objectives and plans. You will also be helping them to examine their motives for choosing a particular course of action in the first place.

All that is fairly straightforward. The difficult part is when you have to be honest – and constructive – by giving them feedback on the negative aspects of themselves. You may have to point out that their objectives are too ambitious for the time being, or to alert them to a negative 'blind spot'.

Giving constructive feedback: dos and don'ts

Do:

▶ Be clear about what you want to say

▶ Start with 'I' when giving your judgement

▶ Start with a positive statement, then move on to the negative

▶ Be specific about the behaviour

▶ Offer alternatives

▶ Be descriptive

Don't:

▶ Waffle round the point

▶ Offer it as a universal opinion

▶ Negate or devalue the whole person

▶ Give general comments

▶ Leave the person with absolutely no idea of how to change their behaviour

▶ Judge

Summary

This section has been a reminder to evaluate and review your progress. You then have to act on your evaluation and update your plans.

Evaluating without acting on the information is like looking to the left and right, before stepping into the road in front of a car.

It is also important to 'reality check' your objectives and plans with another person. Even if they are not telling you anything new, talking things over can help you to put them in perspective.

Above all, don't give up at the first hurdle. The first review is always the worst.

'...the moment you definitely commit yourself,

then Providence moves too.

All sorts of things occur to help you

that would never otherwise have occurred.

A whole stream of events issue from the decision,

raising in your favour all manner of unforeseen incidents and meetings and material assistance,

which no one would have dreamed would come their way.' **GOETHE**

Your personal profile

You will have generated a great deal of information about yourself in the process of seeing where you are, and thinking about your skills and your learning habits. Finding out about yourself can be interesting, but it can also be hard work. You might make good use of the information by putting together a personal profile.

This section will give you suggestions on creating a personal profile, based on current thinking. There are no hard and fast rules as to how to do this, and you may decide to do it another way. However, some guidance on the presentation, content and sequence of the document is provided. It is not a step-by-step guide to a successful CV. It is up to you how you write it, as it has to reflect you – or at least the best side of you. You can use your personal profile in several different ways:

▶ As a basis for your CV

▶ As a basis for an appraisal review

▶ As a basis for discussion about internal promotion

▶ As an accompaniment to your portfolio for accreditation

▶ As a reminder of your achievements and your progress.

The most important principle when compiling a personal profile is:

Put yourself in your reader's place

Write for your audience and check for relevance all the way through by asking yourself 'What would I be looking for in his or her place?'. This principle applies even when you are not writing for a particular person or applying for a particular job. You need to present yourself as positively as possible, making the reading easy and the facts accessible. It can be a tedious job, but it is worth getting it right. The following checklists will help you to do this.

The presentation

▶ Use good, plain white A4 paper, typed on one side only

▶ Don't write – always type or have it typed up for you

▶ Try to make it as short as possible – no more than three pages long

▶ Space it out, with wide margins and one line spaces between paragraphs

▶ Use headings

▶ Keep sentences short and to the point

▶ Watch your spelling

▶ Make it look good: easy to read, easy to see the facts and short.

The sequence

If you were reading a personal profile for any reason, what would you be interested in? Imagine that you are a senior manager reading a three page personal profile. Which items would you be most interested in? Prioritise them according to the page you would like to see them on: one, two, three, or not at all. (This is not a full list.)

▶ Where you were educated

▶ What your first job was

▶ What you have achieved recently

▶ Who you have worked for recently

▶ Your career summary

▶ How many children you have

▶ Your health

▶ Qualifications and courses you have attended

▶ Your less successful moments

▶ Dates of all your qualifications

- ▶ Marital status
- ▶ Place of birth
- ▶ Children's ages
- ▶ Your interests
- ▶ Your name, address and phone number

Suggestions

Page 1:
- ▶ Your name, address and phone number
- ▶ What you have achieved recently
- ▶ Your career summary

Page 2:
- ▶ Who you have worked for recently
- ▶ Qualifications and courses you have attended
- ▶ Your interests

Page 3:
- ▶ Where you were educated
- ▶ Your health
- ▶ What your first job was
- ▶ How many children you have
- ▶ Marital status
- ▶ Place of birth

Not at all:

- Your less successful moments
- Dates of all your qualifications
- Children's ages

Personal profiles often start with a page of details: name, age, marital status, children, educational qualifications, place of birth. But how important is that information compared to recent achievements and responsibilities and your career summary?

Name, address and phone number should go on page 1 (for identification and in case they want to phone you back or write offering you an interview). Other information of that kind is not relevant. Very few people live in the world where the school you went to matters! Who cares about GCSE results and dates if your recent achievements are impressive?

Don't mention your present salary. If you are specifically asked to, mention it in your covering letter.

Mention the fact that references will be supplied if necessary.

Suggested sequence

A suggested sequence, and one that is logical and 'reader-friendly' could be:

- Name
- Address
- Phone number
- Career summary/statement
- Career and achievements to date (working from the present to the past)
- Key skills
- Professional qualifications and training

- ► Education (tertiary followed by secondary: brief outline)
- ► Interests
- ► Personal details (age, marital status, children)

Use a separate page for a client or project list, if you are including one, and make sure it is a list.

The career statement and your achievements

This is possibly the most important part of the profile. Here are some tips:

- ► It needs to be about 20 or so words long
- ► It needs to be angled to sell you and the skills you want to use
- ► State your aspirations – what areas you are interested in and the skills you would like to develop.
- ► Make these tie in with what the reader wants to hear
- ► Imagine that you only have these words to convince your reader of your perfect suitability for the job
- ► You can highlight areas that you are interested in
- ► Leave out the early part of your career if it is irrelevant
- ► Leave out anything irrelevant
- ► It should follow your name and address – the second item on the page
- ► Everything you put into your profile should support your career summary
- ► It focuses the mind – everything in your profile should be relevant to the summary. If it is not, then censor it.

Collect your material

Make a start by making lists under the following headings. You can use them for your career summary and for the bulk of your profile.

Achievements

Use your achievement log – no more than three years old and only relevant ones that will highlight the right areas. Any kind of responsibility or management task looks good.

Skills

Highlight the key skills that fit the position.

Knowledge/professional training

Highlight the relevant skills, courses and qualifications information that you collected in Section 1.

Experience

Use your achievements log and any other relevant experience. It does not have to be an 'achievement' with results. It generally consists of roles and responsibilities and problem solving activities.

Interests

If there is something relevant to the post or something that makes you look good, put that first. Don't leave interests out: they show the kind of person you are. You can give messages about yourself that you can't state overtly. Sport can indicate health and fitness, for example, Early English Plainsong could indicate intellect and canoeing could indicate a pioneering spirit. Be careful, though, don't exaggerate. You may meet a fellow Plainsong expert!

Style of writing

▶ Keep your sentences short and pithy

▶ Use specific and positive action words, eg 'planned', 'produced', 'directed', 'controlled', 'achieved'; and follow them up with facts or a result

▶ Avoid the passive voice, eg 'was planned', 'was produced', 'was directed' (by myself)

▶ Do not use 'I' too much, except in your career statement, where you are stating your aspirations directly. Use bullet points beginning with action words

▶ Give detail: if you are responsible for a team, say how many are in it. If you have responsibility for fact-finding projects or research, say what they are and (very briefly) what you found

▶ If you moved sideways or changed course, say what motivated you to do it (not what motivated you to stop doing the other job).

Now edit your draft

▶ Go though the paragraphs when you have finished the first draft and check for sentences that do not say anything. Cut them out. (You have to be ruthless. Personal profiles are often too long and rarely too short.)

▶ Cut out adjectives, gushing statements, 'very', 'considerable' 'extremely'

▶ Cut out jargon, technical language and 'in' phrases and slogans

▶ Cut out exaggeration

▶ Cut out humour – it is not always read in the way you wrote it and it can be seen as belittling.

Check

▶ Is it about three pages long?

▶ Is it easy to read?

▶ Do you look good?

▶ Do you look positive and enthusiastic?

▶ Do you look interesting?

▶ Would **you** want to meet you?

▶ Give it to someone else to read and ask for feedback.

Collecting evidence for a portfolio

Your portfolio is a collection of evidence of your skills and achievements. You may be putting one together to accompany your profile, or you may be thinking of gaining credit for your competence in the future – completing an NVQ, for instance. Whatever the reason, it is as well to keep it all in one place. A4 ring binders with clear punched polythene sleeves are usually adequate to begin with.

Collecting evidence for an NVQ is a specialised and detailed process. This guide does not address that. However, the principles are the same.

Evidence can include:

▶ Reports

▶ Certificates of achievement

▶ Letters of commendation from clients/managers

▶ Photographs (accompanied by a description of the event or product)

▶ Menus/programmes/marketing literature (accompanied by a description of your role and the events)

▶ Sketches, plans, schedules.

Summary

This section has concentrated on putting together a personal profile, using information from the previous sections. You can use this profile in a number of situations, and keep it updated along with the other logs and plans for future use.

You have also started to collect evidence to make up a portfolio of your work and achievements.

You have set up a system of continuous improvement to help you to:

▶ Improve your present performance

▶ Continue to develop appropriate skills and competence

▶ Realise your full potential

▶ Take charge of your future.

Remember: personal development is a journey, not a destination!

'It's never too late to be what you might have been.'   **GEORGE ELLIOT**

Hawksmere – focused on helping you improve your performance

Hawksmere plc is one of the UK's foremost training organisations. We design and present more than 500 public seminars a year, in the UK and internationally, for professionals and executives in business, industry and the public sector, in addition to a comprehensive programme of specially tailored in-company courses. Every year, well over 15,000 people attend a Hawksmere programme. The companies which use our programmes and the number of courses we successfully repeat reflect our reputation for uncompromising quality.

All our speakers are practitioners who are experts in their own field: as a result, the information and advise on offer at a Hawksmere programme is expert and tried and tested, practical yet up-to-the-minute.

Hawksmere in-company training

In addition to its public seminars Hawksmere works with client companies developing and delivering a wide range of tailored training in industries as diverse as retailing, pharmaceuticals, PR, engineering and service industries.

The emphasis is on working with clients to define objectives, develop content and deliver in an appropriate way. This gives our clients complete flexibility and control.

Hawksmere publishing

Hawksmere publishes a wide range of books, reports, special briefings, psychometric tests and videos. Listed opposite is a selection of key titles.

Desktop Guides

The company director's desktop guide   *David Martin • £15.99*

The company secretary's desktop guide   *Roger Mason • £15.99*

The credit controller's desktop guide   *Roger Mason • £15.99*

The finance and accountancy desktop guide
Ralph Tiffin • £15.99

Masters in Management

Mastering business planning and strategy   *Paul Elkin • £19.99*

Mastering financial management   *Stephen Brookson • £19.99*

Mastering leadership   *Michael Williams • £19.99*

Mastering negotiations   *Eric Evans • £19.99*

Mastering people management   *Mark Thomas • £19.99*

Mastering project management   *Cathy Lake • £19.99*

Mastering personal and interpersonal skills
Peter Haddon • £16.99

Mastering marketing   *Ian Ruskin-Brown • £19.99*

Essential Guides

The essential guide to buying and
selling unquoted companies   *Ian Smith • £25*

The essential guide to business planning and
raising finance   *Naomi Langford-Wood and Brian Salter • £25*

The essential business guide to the Internet
Naomi Langford-Wood and Brian Salter • £19.95

Business Action Pocketbooks

Edited by David Irwin

Building your business pocketbook	£10.99
Developing yourself and your staff pocketbook	£10.99
Finance and profitability pocketbook	£10.99
Managing and employing people pocketbook	£10.99
Sales and marketing pocketbook	£10.99
Managing projects and operations pocketbook	£9.99
Effective business communications pocketbook	£9.99
PR techniques that work	*Edited by Jim Dunn* • £9.99
Adair in Leadership	*Edited by Neil Thomas* • £9.99

Other titles

The John Adair handbook of management and leadership	*Edited by Neil Thomas* • £19.95
The handbook of management fads	*Steve Morris* • £8.95
The inside track to successful management	*Dr Gerald Kushel* • £16.95
The pension trustee's handbook (2nd edition)	*Robin Ellison* • £25
Boost your company's profits	*Barrie Pearson* • £12.99
The management tool kit	*Sultan Kermally* • £10.99
Working smarter	*Graham Roberts-Phelps* • £15.99
Test your management skills	*Michael Williams* • £12.99

The art of headless chicken management
Elly Brewer and Mark Edwards • £6.99

EMU challenge and change – the implications for business
John Atkin • £11.99

Everything you need for an NVQ in management
Julie Lewthwaite • 19.99

Sales management and organisation
Peter Green • £9.99

Hawksmere also has an extensive range of reports and rpecial briefings which are written specifically for professionals wanting expert information.

For a full listing of all Hawksmere publications, or to order any title, please call Hawksmere Customer Services on 0207 881 1858 or fax on 0207 730 4293.

Filofax time management
Specialists in the area of personal
and corporate productivity

The ability to manage time effectively has become a pre-requisite for today's business manager. Essentially professionals need to achieve more from less. They need to improve the quality of their work, complete important work in less time, use fewer resources and work with the full support of their team.

For over 78 years, Filofax, the world leader in personal organisation, has pioneered tools and techniques to help individuals make the most of their time.

Filofax Time Management is the corporate arm of Filofax Group Ltd and offers a flexible solution that is geared specifically towards the business environment.

The Filofax Time Management system is much more than a diary or an organiser, this productive time management tool induces a sense of urgency on high priorities and encourages creative planning. The system is designed to help individuals clarify their goals and focus on priorities, whilst supporting the effective management of meetings, projects and key performance areas.

For your personal copy of the latest product and services catalogue call Filofax on 0990 502230.

In alliance with Hawksmere plc, Filofax Time Management offer training support via public seminars held across the UK. The seminars provide practical guidance in the development of time management skills and teach a pragmatic business philosophy that enables professionals to manage themselves and their time more effectively. Because of its tremedous benefits, we recommend that individuals who use a Filofax Time Management system attend a relevant seminar.

Filofax Time Management is a leading supplier of time management products and training services. Contact them at:

Unit 3, Victoria Gardens
Burgess Hill, West Sussex RH15 9NB
Telephone: 0990 502230 • Fax: 0990 502231
e-mail: timeman@filofax.co.uk